C000016614

MARTIN CRIMP

Martin Crimp was born in London in 1956. Since leaving Cambridge University, where he acted and first began writing for the stage, he has formed close links with the Orange Tree Theatre, Richmond, which has given the first productions of *Living Remains* (1982), *Four Attempted Acts* (1984), *A Variety of Death-Defying Acts* (1985), and *Definitely the Bahamas* (1987) – a highly acclaimed triple-bill directed by Alec McCowen. His fifth play at the Orange Tree – where he was Thames TV Resident Writer during 1988/9 – was *Dealing with Clair* (1988), which starred Tom Courtenay and was directed by Sam Walters. He has been commissioned to write his next play for the Royal Court Theatre, London.

His work for radio includes the Giles Cooper Award winning *Three Attempted Acts* (1985), and the original version of *Definitely the Bahamas*, winner of the 1986 Radio Times Drama Award.

by the same author

Three Attempted Acts
(in *Best Radio Plays of 1985*)
Dealing with Clair

MARTIN CRIMP

play with repeats

NHℬ

NICK HERN BOOKS

A division of Walker Books Limited

A Nick Hern Book

Play with Repeats first published in 1990 as an original
paperback by Nick Hern Books, a division of Walker Books
Limited, 87 Vauxhall Walk, London SE11 5HJ

Play with Repeats copyright © 1990 by Martin Crimp
Front cover illustration:
Bad Faith (Chile) by R.B. Kitaj
from the Collection of the Arkansas Art Center, USA
reproduced by courtesy of the artist and Marlborough Fine
Art (London) Ltd

Set in Baskerville by Book Ens, Saffron Walden, Essex
Printed by Richard Clay Ltd, Bungay, Suffolk

British Cataloguing in Publication Data
  Crimp, Martin, *1956–*
  Play with repeats
  I. Title
  822′.914

ISBN 1-85459-012-X

CAUTION
All rights whatsoever in this play are strictly reserved.
Requests to reproduce the text in whole or in part should
be addressed to the publisher. Application for performance
in any medium or for translation into any language should
be addressed to the author's sole agent, Judy Daish
Associates, 83 Eastbourne Mews, London W2 6LQ.

If you go back now, everything will be the same as before or worse . . . You must understand that chances are limited; no one has unlimited chances. And you never know when you have used your last chance.

Our misfortune is that we crawl about like blind kittens on top of a table, never knowing where the edge is.

PD Ouspensky
Strange Life of Ivan Osokin

PLAY WITH REPEATS

Characters

ANTHONY STEADMAN
NICK/TERRY
KATE/FRANKY
MOUHAMED LAMINE/MAN IN LAUNDERETTE/MARC
MRS DENT/WOMAN AT BUS-STOP/BARBARA

Time and Place

The place is London, but could be any city. The time is best described as the present. The locations are as follows:

ACT ONE   1   THE PUB
                 2   AT LAMINE'S
                 3.1 CUSTOM COILS: THE WORKSHOP
                 3.2 CUSTOM COILS: FRANKY'S OFFICE
                 4   A TEMPORARY BUS-STOP

ACT TWO   1   A LAUNDERETTE
                 2   THE PUB
                 3   CUSTOM COILS: THE WORKSHOP

Note

A pause is denoted throughout by a comma on a separate line. It should no more be ignored than a rest in a musical score may be ignored.

Play with Repeats was written under the Thames Television resident playwright scheme and first presented at the Orange Tree Theatre, Richmond.

Preview: 12 October 1989. Press night: 13 October 1989

The cast was as follows:

ANTHONY STEADMAN	Thomas Wheatley
NICK/TERRY	Stephen Marchant
KATE/FRANKY	Caroline Gruber
MOUHAMED LAMINE/MAN IN LAUNDERETTE/MARC	Ben Onwukwe
MRS DENT/WOMAN AT BUS-STOP/BARBARA	Vivien Heilbron

Director: Sam Walters
Designer: Anne Gruenberg

35, Gb du Vrew Rd
Opposite pub

ACT ONE

1

The pub. TONY *is drinking with* NICK, *who wears his hair in a a ponytail, and* KATE, NICK*'s girlfriend. An electronic fruit-machine is faintly audible in the silences.*

NICK. You want to ask me a question.

TONY. Yes. What is there that you regret?

NICK. What?

TONY. What do you regret?

,

NICK. Nothing.

TONY. What d'you mean nothing?

NICK. I mean nothing.

   KATE *and* NICK *exchange a faint laugh.*

TONY. No, listen: I'm talking about the things you've done in your life.

NICK. Right. So what's wrong with your life?

TONY. No I'm not asking you . . .

NICK. I know that.

TONY. . . . to tell me, to tell me what's wrong with my life.

NICK. I know that.

,

   So let's leave it.

TONY. What I'm asking you is if you've ever regretted anything. Yourself as a person.

NICK. As a person.

TONY. Because I'm not asking you to tell me what's wrong with my life. Because alright I know what's wrong with it. I have insight into that.

NICK. Uh-hu.

,

You're taking it too seriously.

TONY. What?

NICK. You're taking it –

TONY. My life. I'm taking it too seriously.

NICK. You've put your finger on it.

TONY. Well thankyou very much.

,

NICK. There you are.

TONY. Thankyou very much.

NICK. There you are. Look at yourself. You're taking it too seriously.

TONY. Well thankyou. Fuck you as a matter of fact.

NICK. That's fine.

TONY. Fuck you.

,

NICK. My pleasure.

TONY. Because whoever you are . . .

KATE. All the world's a stage.

TONY. . . . you're not in a position to pass judgement.

NICK. Really.

KATE. We're actors. The world's a stage.

TONY. I'm sorry, but that's a meaningless remark.

NICK. She's right.

KATE. We strut. We fret.

NICK. She's right.

TONY. No, I'm sorry but she isn't right. How can that be right? I mean this isn't an act. This is me. I'm here. I'm making decisions. I could've stayed over there where I normally sit but no I've come over here of my own free will to speak to you both because I have something to say. An actor is repeating a part, but this is different, this is entirely different.

,

This is significant. This is me.

KATE. It's a tale told by an idiot.

TONY. Is that supposed to be a comment?

KATE. Signifying nothing.

TONY. Is that supposed to be some kind of a comment?

,

Well is it?

NICK. Leave it.

KATE. It's actually poetry.

NICK. Let's leave it.

TONY. Poetry.

NICK. This is an actress. You're talking to an actress.

,

TONY. What's that – a professional actress?

KATE. I'm Kate. Yes.

TONY. I'm sorry. Hello Kate.

KATE. Hello.

TONY. Anthony. And I apologise. Because I respect your profession.

KATE. Thankyou.

TONY. But as an actress – whatever kind of actress you are – I know that you'll have insight into human nature.

NICK. I'll tell you what I do regret.

,

TONY. Because that's your job.

NICK. I'll tell you what I do regret.

TONY. I'd like you to.

NICK. What I regret, my friend, is the fact that you exist.

KATE *laughs and puts her arm around* NICK.

KATE. He doesn't mean that.

TONY. No that's absolutely fine by me. Because I take that –

NICK. Don't I?

TONY. I take that in the spirit in which it was intended.

NICK. No offence.

TONY. That is to say ie as an example. A trivial example. Absolutely. None taken.

NICK *and* KATE *kiss.* TONY *continues as if he had their attention.*

Because no one's denying, Kate, that we learn from our mistakes. And I accept your point that a poet can turn that into poetry. That's fine. But for the rest of us who are not poets which is the vast majority, by the time we've learned from our mistakes it's already too late. Those opportunities will never return. And even if you study life, even if you write books about it, you can still find yourself in the launderette, not to do your washing, I mean just to keep *warm*.

KATE *slips away.*

Where's she going?

NICK. What d'you mean?

TONY. Katy. Where's Katy going?

NICK. She's going to the toilet.

TONY. OK. Fine.

NICK. She's just going to the toilet.

TONY. No, that's fine.

Listen –

NICK. You have something against that?

TONY. No. Listen. How old am I?

NICK (*shrugs*). Forty?

TONY. How did you know that?

That's exactly right. I'm thirty-nine, and tomorrow I'll be forty.

NICK. Crisis in other words.

TONY. No, are you psychic?

NICK. Congratulations.

TONY. What? No. Not congratulations.

NICK. OK.

TONY. Not congratulations, because . . .

Because. Alright?

NICK. Because.

TONY. Because I will be forty years old tomorrow, and over those forty years, what have I accumulated?

NICK (*shrugs*). Money?

TONY. Money, no.

No I'm not speaking in a material sense.

NICK. Give up.

TONY. Wisdom.

NICK. Wisdom.

TONY. Yes, we accumulate wisdom, but what use is it to us? Because the events when the wisdom would've been useful, they're over and gone.

NICK. Well then that's how it is.

TONY. No that's *not* how it is.

NICK. Well then I'm sorry, I don't understand what you're saying.

TONY. That's alright.

,

No that's alright. I accept that because what I'm trying to say is not rational.

NICK. It's not rational.

TONY. No.

,

NICK. Fine.

TONY. I mean how old are you?

,

NICK. Why? Twenty-eight.

TONY. And what's your profession?

NICK. My profession?

TONY. Yes, what do you do?

NICK. Do I have a job?

TONY. Yes.

NICK (*faint laugh*). No.

TONY. In other words you missed the opportunity. The opportunity was there, but at the crucial moment you said to yourself: this isn't me.

NICK. What opportunity?

TONY. To work. To get a job. Because if that opportunity presented itself again – and what I'm suggesting to you is that that could be possible – you wouldn't say: this isn't me. You'd seize it. You wouldn't be coming here . . .

NICK. I happen to like coming here . . .

TONY. Night after night.

NICK. I like coming here.

TONY. You like coming here.

,

Don't deceive yourself.

KATE *returns.*

Don't deceive yourself. You and Katy here make an attractive couple, as I was saying. But why does an attractive couple come in here night after night to drink this stuff and sit in basically silence?

'

NICK. It's Anthony's birthday.

KATE. Congratulations Anthony.

TONY. Tomorrow. Thankyou.

KATE. Are you doing anything?

TONY. Tomorrow? Not doing as such. No.

As TONY *drains his glass,* KATE *whispers to* NICK.

NICK (*prompted by* KATE). Look, d'you want another drink, Tone?

TONY. Sorry?

NICK. Your birthday. You want a – ?

KATE. Well of course he does.

TONY. A drink? Well yes, if you're . . .

NICK. Pils?

TONY. Holsten Pils. Thankyou very much.

NICK. This dead?

TONY. Thanks. Thanks a lot.

NICK *goes with the empties. Silence punctuated by faint fruit-machine.*

Fantastic. You look fantastic.

KATE *faint laugh.*

TONY. You have a lovely face.

KATE. Thankyou.

TONY. Have I said that before?

KATE. No.

TONY. Because I know I have a habit, I know I've a habit of repeating myself.

KATE. You didn't say that before.

TONY. Good, that's good. You have a lovely face.

KATE. Thankyou.

TONY. You have a lovely face, but you've still failed. Why is that?

KATE (*faint laugh*). I haven't failed.

TONY. Of course you've failed. Look.

KATE. What?

TONY. It's there in your eyes.

'

KATE. Listen, I –

TONY. I didn't want to say that but it's there in your eyes, Kate. What does an actress do in the evenings? An actress works. She's known. I mean Kate what? Kate who? If you weren't here what difference would it make to anything? And naturally you persuade yourself that there is an intention, that it's meant to be like this, it's meant to be. But what does meant to be mean? Meant to be doing the same thing for eighteen years? Meant to be keeping warm next to a clothes-drier while someone writes reports? No way.

'

No way, Kate. Meant to be means nothing.

KATE. What reports?

TONY. Because listen, what are we, you and I?

KATE. Wait a minute, wait a minute. Don't include me in this.

TONY. We're human beings.

KATE. Don't include me.

TONY. We're human beings. And perhaps I'm repeating myself, but for human beings everything should be possible. The language we speak tells us that. It tells us that the potential – by which I mean not only what we could be, but what we might've been – the potential is infinite. And so what's *meant* to happen – which is surely the realisation of that potential – are you with me? – what's meant to happen, hasn't happened. And what *has* happened – what's happened to *us* – was not meant to happen. No.

,

How can we believe that about ourselves? Because listen –

KATE. I'm listening.

TONY. OK.

,

Yes?

KATE. I'm listening to you.

TONY. Good.

KATE. No, I'm interested.

TONY. Well you should be.

KATE. I am. What are you suggesting?

TONY. That's good. Because listen, I normally sit over there and every night I see you, the two of you, over here, and don't you understand my heart bleeds.

KATE. And if I happen to like it here?

TONY. It bleeds for you. What d'you mean: like it here? That's exactly what *he* said. (*Picks up a bottle.*) Don't you know what this stuff is doing to your body? If you got pregnant? What sort of baby you might have?

KATE (*betraying sadness*). That's unlikely.

TONY. Exactly.

,

Yes, exactly.

KATE. So what are you suggesting?

TONY (*intensely*). What I'm suggesting, Kate, is that there is a train. It's going into the tunnel. The children are waving.

,

I'm suggesting that if we could only go *back.*

,

KATE *faint laugh – but the idea is attractive.*

TONY. Yes.

KATE. You can't go back.

TONY. Yes, but if only we could. Live our lives again. Knowing what we do now. Knowing that. Don't you see?

As NICK *approaches with new bottles,* TONY *takes a card from his pocket and passes it to* KATE.

KATE. What's this?

TONY. Look at it. Read it.

KATE. 'Mouhamed Lamine . . .'

TONY. Mouhamed Lamine. Read it.

NICK. Pils.

TONY. Cheers.

KATE. 'Mouhamed Lamine . . .'

NICK. What?

KATE. '. . . African . . .' What's that?

TONY. Marabout.

KATE. 'African Marabout. Psychologist, telepathist, clairvoyant . . .'

NICK. Let's have a look.

KATE. I'm reading. 'Treats all physical and psychological problems. Assures success in business, marriage and competitive sports. Counteracts evil influences . . .'

TONY. Go on.

KATE. 'Action at a distance. Can overcome any problem even if it seems impossible. Results guaranteed. Please bring . . .' What?

TONY. Ring. It's a misprint. Please ring.

KATE. 'Please ring this number any time.'

TONY. That's right.

KATE *and* NICK *examine the card.*

Can I have the card please.

NICK. I'm reading.

TONY. You see: even if it seems impossible.

KATE. So what's 'action at a distance'?

TONY. Spoons, bending spoons. But that's just an example of what can be achieved. Marabout. That means Holy Man.

NICK. Where d'you get this?

TONY. Launderette. I was given it.

TONY *pours some beer. His hand is shaking.*

I just went in there to dry some shirts, and I was given it.

KATE. He wants to go back.

NICK. What, to the launderette?

KATE *laughs.*

TONY. A man like this, he doesn't inhabit the world in a material sense. Meaning he can see.

NICK. See what?

KATE. That everything is possible.

NICK. Oh. Right.

NICK *and* KATE *exchange a glance.*

Of course.

TONY. What, you think I wouldn't?

NICK. Wouldn't what?

TONY. You think I'm weak? Because I'm not weak.

KATE. Wouldn't what?

TONY. What?

KATE. Wouldn't do what?

TONY. Wouldn't ring him. Because I would. I intend to.

NICK. Mr Lamine.

TONY. Yes. Because I'm not afraid.

KATE. Afraid of what? What's he afraid of?

TONY. I'm not afraid.

NICK. I don't know. What *are* you afraid of?

TONY. I'm not.

NICK. Right. So that's OK.

TONY. That's what I'm saying.

NICK. Absolutely.

TONY. Because there's a limit.

NICK. Well absolutely. You've reached it. You've reached your limit.

TONY. Will you give me the card please.

NICK. One moment.

> NICK *produces a plastic teaspoon. He holds it out with ceremony in both hands.*

> Observe.

> *He slowly bends the spoon. It snaps.* KATE *laughs.*

TONY. I don't understand.

NICK. I'm just making a point. (*Ignoring* TONY, *he begins to walk away.*)

TONY. I'd like my card.
Don't just walk away from me!

> TONY *seizes* NICK *who turns and produces a knife.*

You know what you're doing.

NICK. You tell me.

TONY. You're drinking yourself to death . . .

NICK. Am I.

TONY. . . . in here.

,

NICK. Something so trivial.

NICK drops the card and goes to play the fruit-machine. TONY *retrieves it.*

TONY. What's wrong with him?

KATE. Nick? That's just what he's like. So, you're going to ring your friend?

TONY. Who's that?

KATE. Lamine, Mouhamed Lamine. (*Faint laugh.*)

TONY. Why not?

KATE. Why not?

TONY goes to the phone, inserts money and punches the number. His side of the phone-call may form a kind of antiphony with the electronic tunes of the fruit-machine.

TONY. Mr Lamine? – Ah. OK. (*To* KATE.) He's coming. Mr Lamine? – Yes, hello, I'm . . . What it is is I've got one of your cards here and I was wondering . . . – That's right. – That's exactly right. – Well whenever you . . . – No, I work during the day. – Yes, an evening, an evening would be fine. – Now? – Well yes, I suppose, yes I could. – Yes. Thankyou. – Yes I have. – It's here on the card. – No. Fine. That's absolutely fine. – Fifteen minutes. Fourth landing. I've got it. – I'm sorry? – Right. Yes. I look forward to it. (*Hangs up.*) He knew my name.

KATE. What?

TONY. He knew my name: he said I'll see you in fifteen minutes, Mr Steadman.

KATE. Mr what?

TONY. That's my name . . .

KATE. You gave him your name.

TONY. Steadman.

KATE. Come on. You *gave* him your name. I heard you.

She goes and puts her arms around NICK, *turning back to* TONY.

You're drunk. Go home.

TONY. He knew my name.

The fruit-machine spits out money.

Blackout.

2

LAMINE's *room. Subdued light.* TONY *is alone for a few moments, then* MRS DENT *enters. In silence she fastens a piece of string to a hook in the wall and attaches the other end to the back of a chair. The string bisects the stage. She turns to* TONY.

MRS DENT. Mr Lamine will be with you shortly. Please don't touch the string.

MRS DENT *goes.* TONY *contemplates the string.*

LAMINE *enters. Black, blind, and perhaps wearing an anorak, he is not obviously mysterious. He gropes for the string and feels his way along it to the chair before* TONY *speaks.*

TONY. You knew my name.

LAMINE. I'm sorry?

TONY. How did you do that?

'

This isn't what I expected.

LAMINE. That's in the nature of things.

TONY. Right. (*Faint laugh.*)

'

No. Right. I know exactly what you mean.

LAMINE. One day we realise we've spent our lives dreaming. But waking up is difficult.

TONY. I can see that.

LAMINE. You can?

My rate is a pound a minute. I take it you have cash.

TONY. Well I've got –

LAMINE. Fifteen minutes is fifteen pounds, thirty minutes will be thirty. And so on.

TONY. I see.

LAMINE. After sixty minutes that is to say ie one hour, subsequent minutes are half that rate but the minimum unit of charge is then ten minutes or in other words five pounds.

TONY. Right.

LAMINE. You follow.

TONY. You don't think it seems rather –

LAMINE. I'm joking.

TONY. I'm sorry?

LAMINE. I'm joking. I'm not serious. Let me tell you about the idiot who comes to the city. One day an idiot comes to the city for the very first time. He's never seen so many people before, such enormous crowds in constant movement. That night, when his money runs out, he makes his way to Waterloo and finds a broken box to sleep in. But he's afraid that when he wakes up, he won't recognise himself among so many other people. So what the idiot does is he finds a scrap of chalk and makes a mark on the box.

TONY. Chalk.

LAMINE. The mark you see is so that he can identify himself when he wakes up. (*Faint laugh which* TONY *joins in.*) But. But in the night, someone steals the broken box, and crawls into it. So in the morning the idiot wakes up on the ground and the first thing he sees is this man in the box with the chalk mark on it. And he goes up to the other man and he says: Well it's perfectly clear who *you* are – but in that case, who the fuck am *I*?

Big laugh from LAMINE. TONY *joins in uncertainly.*

TONY. Right.

LAMINE. Who the fuck am I.

TONY. No, that's very good.

LAMINE. One day we realise we've spent our lives dreaming, but you can wake up in different ways.

TONY. That's what I want to do.

LAMINE. You want to wake up.

TONY. Yes.

LAMINE. You want to wake up, but at some point in the past.

TONY. Yes. How did you know that?

LAMINE. And why not? If we can imagine it, why shouldn't it be possible?

TONY. That's right. That's basically what I've been saying all evening. But these people, all they can do is trivialise. I mean, why a man has to do that to his hair . . .

LAMINE. I know.

TONY. They're so limited. Just because *they've* failed . . .

LAMINE. I know, I know.

TONY. So he takes out a knife. Any fool can take out a knife.

LAMINE. I know.

In silence LAMINE *feels his way along the string to* TONY. *He raises his hand.*

She's coming.

TONY. Who?

LAMINE. Remind me to tell you the one about death.

TONY. Who's coming?

LAMINE. We both need a drink.

MRS DENT *enters.*

LAMINE. Two Stellas.

MRS DENT *goes.* LAMINE *makes his way back along the string during the following:*

TONY. What I've come to see is that my life –

LAMINE. You're happy with Stella?

TONY. Stella.

LAMINE. Stella Artois. The Carlsberg I'm afraid is finished.

TONY. What, Special Brews.

LAMINE. The Carlsberg Special Brews. They're finished.

TONY. I'm a Pils man.

LAMINE. Holsten Pils.

TONY. Holsten Pils . . . Lowenbrau . . .

LAMINE. I'm sorry we can't offer you a choice.

TONY. I'm happy with Stella.

LAMINE (*raises hand*). She's coming.

TONY. No actually I'm surprised. I thought someone in your position would have to –

LAMINE. My position.

TONY. Yes, would have to abstain.

LAMINE. Abstain?

TONY. Yes.

LAMINE. No. No, that's not necessary.

MRS DENT *enters with beer.*

Mr Steadman would like me to abstain. (MRS DENT *laughs softly.*) Mrs Dent is my eyes, aren't you, Mrs Dent. She is my eyes, and at times, my feet.

MRS DENT. I told him not to touch the string.

LAMINE. I don't think he would touch the string.

LAMINE *and* TONY *open cans.* MRS DENT *lingers.*

MRS DENT. Mr Lamine, there are some people –

LAMINE. Tell them to go away.

MRS DENT. It's that woman –

LAMINE. I know.

MRS DENT. It's that woman who lost her baby.

LAMINE. I know, I know. Tell her to go away.

MRS DENT *goes.*

I'm sorry. There are some things I'm not prepared to do.

They drink.

TONY.   } I feel very –
LAMINE. } People think –

TONY. Sorry.

LAMINE. No. Go on.

TONY. You were –

LAMINE. No. Please go on.

,

TONY.   } I wanted to –
LAMINE. } Please –

TONY. What?

LAMINE. Please go on.

TONY. I wanted to say –

LAMINE. You must go on.

TONY. Yes, to say . . . just to say: I feel very . . . relaxed here. It isn't what I imagined.

LAMINE. Relaxed.

TONY. Yes.

LAMINE. Good.

,

Good. Is that all?

TONY. No. Well no. Obviously . . . (*Decisive.*) Two things.

LAMINE. Good.

TONY. The first . . .
Well look I have a particular way of folding my shirts . . .
No, let me go back a bit.
What I'm trying to say is, is I live on my own as it were,
which is fine, which is absolutely fine, as far as it goes. I
mean it's something that I have insight into. Because it's
something that's happened largely out of choice. And I
mean the room itself limits, largely limits what I do,
because of its size. Because if I were to invite somebody
back – let's say from the pub – then it would be
embarrassing, the size of the room being such that . . .
you would be too close to the other person at any given
time. They would question your motives. So in a sense
the room itself imposes certain limits, which I accept. It's
certainly very convenient for me. Just a bus-ride from my
job. And I have a range of appliances. And the toilet is a
reasonable distance. I mean it's not so close that you
hear everyone else, but it's not so far away that you have
to make other arrangements, d'you see what I mean. The
microwave has made a big difference, naturally. It means
you're completely your own master when it comes to
meals. You can have a hot meal any time although in
practice I tend to eat at quarter past six and maybe a
little earlier at weekends. So what I'm saying is, is I have
insight into that. I can see myself folding my shirts and I
realise I do it in a particular way which I'd be loath to
change. But then I met Heather, and –

LAMINE. Who is . . .

TONY. Heather? Right. Yes. Sorry.

LAMINE. Don't be.

TONY. No. I'm sorry.

LAMINE. Don't be.

Heather.

TONY. Yes. Heather is . . . No, this is the whole point.
Because some time ago, Heather and I . . . I met
Heather. And with Heather. You see this is something
I've never been able to do before, to initiate a
relationship –

LAMINE. This is a physical relationship.

TONY. Physical. Yes. Certainly physical. But more than
   that. Undoubtedly physical, but more than that it's . . .
   Yes, exactly what you were saying. It's like waking up,
   but when you look out of the window, instead of the
   Complex . . .

LAMINE. Which is . . .

TONY. There's a Leisure Complex at the back of us and
   we're always in its shadow. But instead of that it's as if
   there's a landscape . . .

LAMINE. Opening up.

TONY. Yes. How did you know that? It's opening up.
   That's right. And what I saw was the possibility of
   another life. Not this. Not this life. But the possibility . . .
   I don't know . . . of love . . . an act of love . . . starting a
   family . . . not this life.

,

But you see – and of course I know this now – what I
   did – and I did this in good faith – but what I did was,
   which is what I regret, was I failed to assert myself.
   Because in respecting her – which I do, which I still do –
   as a person, I realise now I didn't give her the necessary
   attention as a woman. I didn't assert myself as a man.

LAMINE. She was afraid of you.

TONY. That's right.

,

That's exactly right. Terrified. How did you know?

LAMINE. And this went on for how long?

TONY. Sorry?

,

No, we met once. Only this once. Just by chance. At a
   bus-stop.

LAMINE. A bus-stop.

TONY. A temporary bus-stop.

LAMINE. And the second?

TONY. I'm sorry?

LAMINE. There were two things.

TONY. Of course, yes. I . . .

LAMINE (*raises hand*). She's coming.

TONY. What, shall I . . .

LAMINE. No. Please go on.

TONY. No, the other thing is my job.

> MRS DENT *enters softly during the following and picks up the ring-pulls.*

Because alright, I've been doing the same thing – which is winding coils – for eighteen years now. Yes. Eighteen years. I wind coils for loudspeakers, quality loudspeakers, which in itself is not something I regret. On the contrary I have the satisfaction – which is why I've never gone in for office work – the satisfaction of possessing a skill, and knowing that because of that skill I've made myself indispensable, ie this is something that not many people can say about themselves. Whereas the others – Terry for example – is not what you'd call skilled and he makes a lot of sexual remarks which I would find offensive as a woman. But what I'm getting at *is*, is you would've thought – and correct me if I'm wrong – but you would've thought that someone with eighteen years experience . . . Because when Barry left with his heart they needed a new Supervisor, and the essential thing here is that I wasn't even told the job was *advertised*. No. By the time I found that out – which in itself was purely a matter of chance – they'd already appointed someone else – Marc – who happens to be black – which I only mention – because we get on very well – but the fact remains that his previous place of employment was a Pizza Hut.

What I should've done – and of course I see this now so clearly – is the moment Barry left, I shouldn't've waited, I should've gone to personnel, I should've spoken to Franky, who is an intelligent girl, and I should've seized that opportunity. After all it's not as if I'm frightened of Franky, (*Faint laugh.*) who is in fact younger than myself. It's not as if I don't have every reason to go in there and ask her for what is mine by rights. Surely.

,

It's not fear. It's . . .

,

You see this is something I was destined to do.

MRS DENT. That's an odd choice of words.

TONY. Look, I'm sorry, does she have to –

LAMINE. Mrs Dent is my eyes.

MRS DENT. It's just a comment.

TONY. I'm not asking for comments.

,

I'm not asking for comments. I mean what exactly is her role in this?

MRS DENT. Mouhamed found my husband. He'd gone off and taken the children. What he'd done was he'd locked them in a room. (*She takes* LAMINE's *hand. She begins to weep.*) Mouhamed saw the room. He could see them in the room. He could describe them. He could describe their faces.

LAMINE *comforts her. Excluded by this private grief,* TONY *finally speaks to draw attention to himself.*

TONY. I'm not asking for comments.

LAMINE. You're asking to go back.

TONY. Yes. Knowing what I do now.

LAMINE. And this is what you want.

TONY. It's what I came here for.

LAMINE. If that's what you want, no problem.

TONY. No problem.

LAMINE. No problem.

,

If that's what you want.

TONY. You keep saying that.

LAMINE. Well – OK.

'

TONY. So, what, there's some kind of . . . procedure?

LAMINE. Procedure?

MRS DENT. There is no procedure.

'

TONY. Right. Meaning . . .

LAMINE. That's it.

TONY. Meaning that's it. OK.

'

LAMINE. OK?

TONY. Thankyou.

LAMINE. Provided of course you believe that it's possible.

TONY. I wouldn't be here, Mr Lamine –

LAMINE. Because there are some people – aren't there – they ask me to bend a spoon and I bend a spoon. But they look at the spoon and they say: this spoon is straight.

TONY. No, that's exactly right. I understand that mentality.

LAMINE. This spoon is straight.

TONY. The pub where I drink, that's exactly the mentality.

LAMINE. Christ could appear in the garden.

TONY. This spoon is straight. That's just what they'd say.

LAMINE. He could appear in the garden and exhibit his wounds.

TONY. Well that's right.

LAMINE. Jesus Christ could appear.

TONY. I know. That's exactly –

LAMINE (*very lightly*). Let me tell you the one about death.

'

A man is queueing up in a cafeteria at Kings Cross
Station when he notices death a little way ahead of him,
paying for a ham and salad sandwich. Overwhelmed by
panic he slips out of the queue, replaces his tray,
withdraws all his money from the bank and flies
immediately to a Greek Island. Later in the day death
happens to be chatting to one of the man's friends in the
Farringdon Road. Where is so-and-so these days, says
death. Oh, says the friend, he'll be hanging round a
station or sitting in a pub somewhere. He's a bit cautious
and he never goes far. Well that's what I thought, says
death, but the thing is, is he's down here on my list, and
in a couple of days time I'm due to collect him from
Corfu of all places. (*He laughs.*) Corfu of all places.

LAMINE *continues to laugh, joined by* MRS DENT, *who has
been winding up the string during the latter part of this story.*
TONY *also laughs, uncertainly.*

TONY. No. Corfu. That's very good.

Blackout.

3.1

Custom Coils. Harsh light. Loud music. TONY *and* TERRY *are
working. They both wear a kind of surgical hat whose function is
more symbolic than practical.* TONY *has his back to the room, and
in addition to the hat he wears ear-cans to block out the noise of the
radio. Nothing for some time except light and noise. Then* FRANKY,
*the personnel manager, enters. She crosses the room to collect some
documents, unnoticed by* TONY, *but immediately attracting*
TERRY's *attention. Only fragments of the following are audible.*

TERRY. Looks to me like someone was up last night.
   Tell him he can put one in for me next time.
   If you're not getting the satisfaction you need love, just
   let me know. Satisfaction's my middle name.
   If you like music come round some time and have a go
   on my equipment.
   You just let me know.
   First the mashed potatoes, then the gravy.

Oblivious to this, **FRANKY** *goes out with the documents.*

TERRY. Hey Tony. FIRE! FIRE! EARTHQUAKE! END OF THE FUCKING WORLD!

TERRY laughs. **TONY** *of course hears none of this, but as if sensing something he turns round slowly and discovers* **TERRY** *laughing.* **TONY** *also laughs, uncertainly, attempting to share the joke, before turning back to his work.*

(*Unvoiced, without rancour.*) Fucking idiot.

FRANKY enters again. The music persists.

FRANKY. Mr Steadman. Mr Steadman.

No response from **TONY.** *TERRY laughs, shakes his head.*

Mr Steadman.
Will you turn that off, Terry. Turn it off. Now.

TERRY laughs, pretends not to understand, but complies. Silence.

Mr Steadman.

TERRY. If you want his attention Franky love, you'll have to put your hand down his trousers.

FRANKY. Will you shut up.

TERRY. On second thoughts, put it down mine and I'll pass on the message. (**FRANKY** *looks at him.*) Joke, Franky.

,

Joke.

TONY, *sensing something, turns and sees* **FRANKY.** *He removes the ear-cans.*

FRANKY. Mr Steadman.

TONY. Yes. Sorry. Have you been trying to –

FRANKY. There was a note. There was a note saying you wanted to see me.

TERRY. Go for it Tony.

TONY. What?

TERRY. Joke.

,

Joke.

TONY. That's right. If it's convenient.

FRANKY. Fine.

She waits.

TONY. No, it's just that . . .

FRANKY. No, that's fine. I understand. Let's say in my office in two minutes, shall we.

TONY. Right. Thanks.

TERRY. Steady on, Tony.

TONY. Two minutes then.

FRANKY. Fine.

TERRY. You don't know what forces you're unleashing there, my love. I mean what we're basically talking about here is a man who gets a hard-on when he touches your coffee cup.

TONY. Hey, leave it out.

TERRY. Which he does frequently.

FRANKY *has gone. Both men faint laugh.* TONY *is embarrassed but flattered by this reference to his 'virility'. Silence.*

So you want Barry's job?

TONY. What?

TERRY. I said you want –

TONY. That's right.

TERRY. Barry's job.

She won't give you that.

TONY. Uh-hu. She won't.

TERRY. She won't give you Barry's job.

TONY. Well we'll see.

Won't we. We'll see about that.

TERRY. And I'll tell you why.

,

I'll tell you why.

TONY. What d'you know about it?

TERRY. I'll tell you why.

TONY. Because in point of fact you don't know what you're talking about.

TERRY. Don't I.

TONY. Well you tell me.

TERRY. Don't I, mate.

TONY. You tell me then.

,

You tell me why.

TERRY. I'll tell you why.

TONY. Fine that's fine. Do so.

TERRY. I'll tell you why, and the reason is she's frigid.

,

Exactly.

TONY. Come on . . .

TERRY. She is basically frigid. You could go in that office. You could give her mashed potatoes and gravy. And you still wouldn't get Barry's job. And d'you know why?

TONY (*gets out a newspaper cutting*). You see, look at this.

TERRY. D'you know why: because she would feel nothing. Butter wouldn't melt, mate.

TONY. No, look at this.

TERRY. So what's this? (*He turns the paper in his hand, affecting indifference.*)

TONY. Well you can see what it is.

TERRY. I know what it *is*.

,

I mean I don't need you to tell me what it *is*.

TONY. So this time I'm going to ask for an explanation.

TERRY (*passing back the paper*). Yea, you should.

TONY. You think?

TERRY. Something like that, you definitely should.

,

That Christmas party I could've had her.

TONY. Had who?

,

TERRY. He asks who.

TONY (*faint laugh*). Franky?

TERRY. He asks who. Of course Franky.

TONY. But weren't you . . . I thought you were –

TERRY. I could've had her. Don't tell me I couldn't.

TONY. OK.

TERRY. Don't tell me I couldn't alright. Because the fuck –

TONY. OK.

TERRY. The fuck you know about it.

,

Which is how I know.

,

TONY. How you know what?

TERRY. How I know. Because she was up against that wall.
She was up against that boardroom wall, and believe me
she wanted it.

TONY. Alright.

TERRY. Whatever she *says*.

,

TONY. What does she say?

TERRY. She doesn't *say* anything. She wouldn't, would she.

But she doesn't have to. Because she knows. And she knows that next time it will be different.

TONY. Uh-hu.

TERRY. Whatever she *says*.

They fall silent. TERRY *produces a gift-wrapped bottle and tosses it to* TONY.

TONY. What's this?

TERRY. Happy returns, that's all.

TONY (*moved*). Thanks. Thanks a lot.

TERRY. We do what we can.

TONY. No. Really. How did you know?

TERRY. Barbara knew.

TONY. Did she? So is she coming in?

TERRY. No, she phoned. She can't.

'

TONY. A gift. This has never happened before.

FRANKY enters.

FRANKY. If you'd like to come in now.

TONY *stands, removes hat.*

TONY. Right. (*To* TERRY.) Thankyou very much.

TERRY. Put one in for me, Tony.

Blackout.

3.2

FRANKY's *office.* TONY *nurses the present. Silence.* FRANKY *is not of course the cold stereotype of* TERRY's *imagining. Throughout what follows her concern is to do what's best for* TONY.

TONY. Listen, I'm sorry about –

FRANKY. Don't worry about Terry. If this organisation was

slightly larger we'd be *obliged* to employ a certain number of mentally handicapped people.

Both faint laugh.

Today's your birthday.

TONY. That's right.

FRANKY. Congratulations.

TONY. Thankyou.

FRANKY. Are you doing anything?

TONY. Sorry? No. No I'm not.

,

Not doing as such.

FRANKY. What did you want to see me about?

TONY. Right. OK. Yes. (*Decisive.*) Two things.

FRANKY. Two things. Fine.

TONY. Yuh. No. What am I saying? One.

FRANKY. One thing. That's fine.

TONY. I'm not making myself –

FRANKY. You are. Perfectly clear.

TONY. Am I?

FRANKY. Perfectly.

TONY. Right.

,

TONY. Right, the thing is – this is what's confusing – is last time this happened –

FRANKY. Last time what happened?

TONY. Ah. No. You wouldn't – of course you wouldn't – you wouldn't be aware of that.

FRANKY. I'm not.

TONY. No.

Both faint laugh.

No. Forget that.

FRANKY. Fine.

TONY. I digress. (*Faint laugh*.)

FRANKY. No that's fine. What did you want to see me
about?

TONY (*intensely*). I want Barry's job. Barry's left. I want his
job.

FRANKY. Uh-hu . . .

TONY. That's it. I want his job.

,

FRANKY. This is the . . .

TONY. The supervising job, that's right.

He takes out the newspaper cutting.

Because look: this is . . .
What I'm trying to say is, is I only came across this by
chance, Franky – Miss Wood – by chance –

FRANKY. Franky's fine.

TONY. Purely by chance. Purely by chance I come across
an advertisement for this job – because no one has
approached me – I find an advertisement for something
which is by rights mine. And all I'm trying to say is, is
how would *you* feel, is why wasn't my attention directed
to this?

FRANKY. Listen, we're obliged to advertise.

TONY. I realise you're obliged. I accept that. But why
wasn't I approached? Because everybody knows that
when you do that – when you advertise – that's just to
cover yourself – so you cover yourself – and then you
appoint your man from the inside.

FRANKY. Not necessarily.

TONY. No.

,

No. Agreed. Not necessarily, but this is my job.

FRANKY. You can certainly apply.

TONY. Something that is mine by rights.

FRANKY. You can apply.

TONY. You keep saying that. You keep saying that: apply. But no way am I going to compete.

,

No way. Because I can compete and I know what will happen: what will happen is what happened before.

FRANKY. Before what?

TONY. And it won't happen again.

,

FRANKY. Before what?

TONY. Something I'm quite clearly destined to do.

FRANKY. That's an odd choice of words.

TONY. Well I'm sorry.

FRANKY. In the context. I just mean in what amounts to a fairly trivial context.

TONY. Well I'm sorry about the context, but the context is my life.

FRANKY. That's not what I meant.

TONY. And I'm sorry if it happens to be trivial.

FRANKY. That's not what I meant.

The phone rings.

Look, I didn't realise you'd feel so strongly about this.

TONY. Well I do, Miss Wood. I feel very strongly.

FRANKY. D'you mind if I take this call.

She answers the phone.

Custom Coils. Frances Wood speaking. – Right, will you tell him I'm in a meeting. – I should think about two more minutes. – OK. Thanks.

She hangs up. Silence.

No one is questioning your skill, Tony.

TONY. Good. Thankyou.

FRANKY. But this isn't the same kind of job. This is about managing people.

TONY. Right. Human nature.

'

Human nature, I have insight into that.

FRANKY. Fine, that's fine. Barbara in today?

TONY. No. Apparently she phoned.

FRANKY. What, she's depressed?

TONY. I should think so. She usually is.

FRANKY. She has to be watched.

TONY (*faint laugh*). That time she cut her wrists . . .

FRANKY. Which time are we talking about?

TONY. The third time: the third time when she cut them at home and then came into work on the bus. (*Faint laugh.*) That's a half hour journey. Only Barbara could do that.

FRANKY. I know.

TONY. Well it's a cry for help of course. It's not actually serious. It's just that particular time, the blood . . .

FRANKY. She has to be watched.

TONY. That's right. And the tears. Every day there are tears . . .

FRANKY. She'll destroy things to get your attention.

TONY. Well that's right.

FRANKY. There's Terry . . .

'

TONY. Destroy things. No, you're absolutely right about her.

FRANKY. There's Terry. Now you probably realise what Terry wants . . .

TONY. I know. It must be embarrassing for you. No, if I

was responsible I'd put a stop to that. You see it's ever
since the Christmas party . . .

FRANKY. The Christmas party.

>

What d'you mean, the Christmas party?

TONY. Well ever since –

FRANKY. Ever since what? I'm not talking about his
imagination. I'm talking about the fact that what he
needs, is someone to permanently hold his hand.

TONY (*nods*). Hold his hand, right.

FRANKY. Hold his hand. Because you must know for
example that Terry can't read or write.

>

You do know that?

TONY. Uh-hu.

>

Read or write. But he seems to –

FRANKY. Yes he manages . . .

TONY. Because he seems to manage . . .

FRANKY. Yes he manages, but the reason he manages, is
because Barry's always helped him. Barry explains the
orders. Barry fills in his time-sheet. He brings in a paper
and tells Terry what's going to be on television.
Sometimes he writes letters for him. This is quite apart
from his actual *work*.

TONY. Uh-hu.

FRANKY. OK? I just want to make sure you realise what
can be involved.

The phone's ringing.

TONY. It just makes you wonder –

FRANKY. D'you mind if I take this.

She answers the phone.

Custom Coils. Frances Wood speaking. – Yes. OK. I'm

still in a meeting. – Tell him I'll be with him in one
minute. – OK. Thanks. (*She hangs up*.)

TONY. It makes you wonder why you employ people like
that.

Faint laugh from FRANKY. *She lights a cigarette. Silence.*

FRANKY. Look, you can have the job.

TONY. Yuh?

No. I'm amazed.

FRANKY. If that's what you want.

TONY. It's what I came in here for, Miss Wood.

FRANKY. Franky.

TONY. Franky.

FRANKY. Well – OK.

TONY. I'm amazed.

FRANKY. Don't be amazed.

TONY. I am. I'm amazed.

FRANKY. If that's what you want.

TONY (*laughing*). Thankyou.

FRANKY (*laughing*). Don't thank me.

TONY. No. Thankyou.

FRANKY. Because obviously you feel strongly, and if that's
what you want . . .

TONY. You keep saying that.

FRANKY. . . . then it's yours.

TONY. You keep saying that.

Because –

FRANKY. No, that's fine.

TONY. I'm amazed.

FRANKY. It's a good opportunity for you.

TONY. Well that's right.

,

It is. And I knew that this time if I just . . . put myself forward, asserted myself. If I actually came to you –

FRANKY. Well you have. I'm very pleased.

TONY. Because I'm thinking of starting a family.

FRANKY. Well I'm very pleased for you.

,

Now look . . .

TONY. I don't believe this.

FRANKY. Look, I can't immediately put my hands on the details . . .

TONY. That's not a problem.

FRANKY. Obviously the conditions of service will be exactly the same . . .

TONY. Right.

FRANKY. No union membership.

TONY. Right. Yes.

FRANKY. After two more years continuous service, there'll be another day's annual holiday.

TONY. Right.

FRANKY. Obviously you'll be on the next pay increment.

TONY. Right. Good.

FRANKY. We'll have to advertise your present job obvi–

TONY. Obviously. Right.

FRANKY. And you will need to apply in writing for this one.

TONY. Formality. I understand that.

FRANKY (*terminating interview*). Right.

,

TONY. That's it.

FRANKY. That's it.

TONY. There's no . . .

FRANKY. What?

TONY. There's no . . .

FRANKY. Probationary period? Absolutely not. No, we'll just put you straight in at that grade.

TONY. OK.

FRANKY. OK?

The phone's ringing.

Fine. I must . . .

TONY. I'll see myself out.

FRANKY *answers the phone.* TONY *heads for the door, but turns back and waits in the room.*

FRANKY. Custom Coils. Frances Wood. – Yes, put him through. – Geoffrey, yes, I'm sorry. – I know. – Yes I know. We're going to have to change that procedure. – Well basically what they're doing is clocking each other's cards. – I know. – Yes I realise that, but you know as well as I do Geoffrey that if you pay peanuts you end up with monkeys, it's as simple as that. – (*Laughs.*) I've got nothing at all against monkeys. – Yes I've seen the programmes, Geoffrey. I know they can. (*Laughs.*)

She notices that TONY *is still in the room.*

Listen, while you're there, would you take out the three centimetre semi-display we have in the Standard. – Yes, the post is filled. – Since today. – What? – I'm working after work. That's what I'm doing. – Yes. Work. How's your wife? – (*Laughs.*) Is she? – (*More laughter.*) I don't believe you, Geoffrey. – Alright. Goodbye.

FRANKY *hangs up, laughs quietly, inviting* TONY *to share her amusement, but finds him preoccupied.*

What can I do for you?

TONY. You're right.

FRANKY. I'm sorry?

TONY. What you said. Terry. Barbara. Then there'll be a new person. It's not for me.

FRANKY. OK.

,

Are you –

TONY. I'm sorry. It's not fear.

,

(*With contempt.*) I'm not frightened of *them*.

,

It's not the responsibility because I want the responsibility. I can't explain.

FRANKY. That's OK. I understand.

TONY. It's not me.

,

That's all. It isn't me. Is it?

,

Well is it?

FRANKY. I can't say. How can I say?

,

I don't think so. No.

TONY. No.

FRANKY. But listen you're welcome to think –

TONY. I don't want to think. Thankyou. No I don't want to think.

FRANKY. I understand.

TONY. It's not me. This isn't me.

,

FRANKY. I understand.

TONY. You keep saying that.

,

You keep saying that.

Blackout.

4

A temporary bus-stop. Night. TONY *stands holding his present. Also waiting is a* WOMAN *of similar age. They exchange a brief glance and smile. Silence. When their eyes meet again they begin to speak.*

WOMAN. Are you waiting for –

TONY. A three-three-nine, that's right.

Both faint laugh.

TONY. We may as well sleep here.

WOMAN. I'm sorry? (*Faint laugh.*) Yes.

TONY. Joke.

WOMAN. I know. I'm sorry.

TONY. No, I'm sorry . . .

WOMAN. No you're right.

'

You're absolutely right. It's only you meet . . .

TONY. I frightened you.

WOMAN. No, it's only you meet . . . Sometimes late at night . . .

TONY. You can meet some pretty weird people late at night.

WOMAN. Yes.

Both faint laugh.

I don't know why they've had to move the stop somewhere so dark.

TONY. It's only temporary.

WOMAN. D'you think it will be permanently like this?

'

Some friends from the Institute were meant to be giving me a lift, but –

TONY. But they buggered off.

WOMAN. How did you guess.

Both faint laugh.

No really . . .

TONY. Human nature . . .

WOMAN. . . . how did you know that?

TONY. What Institute is that? Is that the –

WOMAN. I go to classes there. Crossley Road.

TONY. Uh-hu.

WOMAN. I'm involved in various things.

TONY. Uh-hu. Is that right.

,

So what sort of things are various things?

WOMAN. Well, for example, there's History.

TONY. That's fascinating.

WOMAN. This term it's the twentieth century.

,

TONY. No, that's fascinating. The twentieth century. That's . . .

WOMAN (*dispassionate list*). Vietnam. The Holocaust. The Atom Bomb of course. Then we go back to the Spanish Civil War. Guernica. And of course we've done the Somme, the battle of the Somme . . .

TONY. That's a picture, isn't it.

WOMAN. Sorry?

TONY. Guernica is a picture.

WOMAN. Is it?

,

Of course Lawrence uses a lot of visual material. Photographs. Films.

TONY. Lawrence being . . .

WOMAN. Lawrence is our tutor.

,

TONY. So, what, you memorise . . .

WOMAN. Memorise?

TONY. Memorise the dates.

WOMAN. We try to memorise the dates. But Lawrence
doesn't really like us doing that. He's very keen on
making us think. He says he doesn't care if we've been
working all day long, we still mustn't accept what's
happened without thinking about why. Why why why.
He gets quite angry. (*Faint laugh.*) He's actually quite
attractive.

TONY. Is he?

WOMAN. You might've heard of him. Bott. Lawrence Bott.

TONY. Lawrence Bott.

,

No. (*Vague recollection.*) No, actually it is familiar.

WOMAN. He's just published a book.

,

TONY. So what's he been getting angry about tonight?

WOMAN. Tonight? No. Sorry. Tonight was French.
Tuesdays is French.

TONY. Right. Bonjour Mademoiselle.

Both faint laugh.

WOMAN. What's that?

TONY. It's French.

WOMAN. I know, but what does it mean?

TONY. Bonjour Mademoiselle? Well it's . . . hello. It just
means hello.

WOMAN. We haven't done that yet. What we're doing this
term is we're just making the sounds. It has some
beautiful sounds.

TONY. The language of love.

WOMAN. You don't go –

TONY. To classes? No, but . . .

WOMAN. But I suppose you have interests.

TONY. Well what interests me is human nature.

WOMAN. Human nature is fascinating.

TONY. Because you can go to classes. That's one way and I respect that. But the other way is to sit tight. You observe. You compare. You don't do anything as such. But you analyse. You analyse and over the years you find that what you accumulate . . .

WOMAN. Is wisdom.

TONY. Yes.

Both smile. TONY*'s increasing self-confidence has a mesmerising effect on the woman.*

Hold this a minute. (*He gives her the present.*)

WOMAN. D'you know who you're like: you're very like Lawrence.

TONY. Am I?

TONY *presses his fingers to his temples.*

WOMAN (*amused*). What're you doing?

TONY. Heather.

WOMAN. How d'you know that?

TONY. Heather. Your name is Heather.

WOMAN. How did you do that?

TONY *laughs.*

WOMAN (*laughs*). No, how did you do that?

TONY. Heather. That's your name.

WOMAN. Yes.

TONY. Your name is Heather.

WOMAN. I know. Yes. Are you psychic?

TONY. What's mine?

WOMAN (*laughs*). I've no idea.

TONY. You don't know my name?

WOMAN. No. Are you famous?

TONY. Anthony. Anthony Steadman. No I'm not famous.

WOMAN. Well hello Anthony.

TONY. Hello Heather.

They laugh and shake hands. HEATHER *moves away, rubbing her bare arms. Silence. Then.*

HEATHER. Have I met you somewhere?

TONY. You're cold. (*He takes off his jacket.*)

HEATHER. No, it's nothing.

TONY. No, you're cold. Your arms are cold. Come on.

HEATHER *acquiesces and he helps her into the jacket.*

It's because the sky's clear. It gets cold when the sky's clear.

HEATHER. I must look like an idiot in this . . . Some kind of scarecrow. (*Laughing, she 'models' the jacket.*)

TONY. No. Fantastic. You look fantastic.

HEATHER. What is this anyway? (*ie the present which she holds.*)

TONY. You really do.

HEATHER. What is this?

TONY. For you. Open it.

HEATHER. But it's yours.

TONY. No. Go on. Open it.

She starts to unwrap.

It suits you.
You see there are two things. One it's my birthday. Two I've been promoted.

HEATHER. I think someone's had this before you. It's half empty.

TONY. What?

HEATHER. I said I think someone's –

TONY. Yes I heard you. What d'you mean?

HEATHER. Look.

TONY takes the bottle, which is less than half-full.

So . . . it sounds like you've got a lot to celebrate.

TONY. What's this supposed to mean?

HEATHER. Congratulations.

TONY. I mean is this supposed to be some kind of a comment?

HEATHER. Someone's made a mistake, that's all.

TONY. Terry.

HEATHER. That's not something you could do intentionally.

TONY. Because Terry can keep it.

HEATHER. It's not important is it?

'

TONY. No. I'm sorry.

HEATHER. Terry. Is that . . . is that a girl's name?

TONY. A girl? No. Terry . . . How would you describe Terry? He's just . . . one of my employees. We're obliged you see to take on a certain number of mentally handicapped people.

HEATHER. That's very humane.

TONY. Yes.

Silence. Then both faint laugh.

Look in the pockets.

HEATHER. What?

TONY. No, have a look. (*She feels in the jacket pockets, while he opens the bottle.*) This time I'm prepared.

HEATHER *discovers two paper cups. She laughs.*

HEATHER. Did you *plan* this? You know, I don't normally drink spirits.

TONY (*pouring drinks*). Neither do I. I drink lager as a rule, premium lager. Cheers.

HEATHER. Cheers. To us.

TONY. To us.

Both drink. TONY *immediately refills his cup.*

HEATHER. Have I met you somewhere?

TONY. You've never married.

HEATHER. Sorry?

TONY. You've never –

HEATHER. No. Married? No.

TONY. I haven't.

HEATHER. Is that a matter of principle?

TONY. Absolutely not. No.

HEATHER. You see I'm not against marriage. But interestingly enough that's an area where Lawrence and I, we part company. Because Lawrence, he's a very right-on sort of person, and –

TONY. What's that? What's right-on?

HEATHER. Well it means . . . I suppose it means he's basically to the left . . .

TONY. Uh-hu . . .

HEATHER. And as someone who is basically to the left – which I respect him for that – but he feels that a woman shouldn't let herself be defined –

TONY. This is what Lawrence feels . . .

HEATHER. Yes. Shouldn't let herself – historically speaking – be defined in terms of her sexual role ie wife, mistress, mother. He says it's degrading. And in our class we have these discussions where we clash. (*Faint laugh.*) Lawrence and I always clash, because I say to him –

TONY. Right. (*He takes the bottle.*)

HEATHER. Look, Lawrence, a woman can't turn her back
on her sexuality any more than a man can. She can't
become neutral. Because isn't that neutrality equally
degrading? You can't ignore what you biologically are.
(As TONY *refills her cup.*) Just a little.
But Lawrence disputes that. (*Faint laugh.*) I think –
although of course I shouldn't say this – but I think
perhaps he has an ethnic problem.

Silence. HEATHER *wraps the jacket around herself.*

This is warm. Thankyou.

Did you read that thing?

TONY. What thing is that?

HEATHER. It was just a thing. I read this thing where two
tourists, there were two tourists, on a beach, it was on a
Greek island, this is a crowded beach, and what they did
was they just started to make love, I mean in front of
everyone, on a crowded beach.

TONY. That's offensive.

HEATHER. But I don't think that it *is*, Anthony. You see I
think we have to admit what we biologically are. That
some things may simply be inevitable. But of course
Lawrence disputes that. (*She drinks.*) And it's the same
with children.

TONY. I like children.

HEATHER. So do I. I love them, because they're innocent
and they're the future. But Lawrence won't hear about
the future. He says: look at the world, what right do we
have to a future? And each week he turns out the lights
and he shows us films: cities in ruins, or human bodies
being bulldozed into graves. Which is all very well.
Which is all very well but we still have a right. Because
each generation, each child, is another life. Is a chance to
escape from that.

TONY. I know exactly what you mean.

HEATHER. Just because one generation, one life, has

failed, doesn't mean that the next one will. That's not logical.

TONY. No.

HEATHER. And besides I think we all as human beings have a duty to direct people's attention away from all that ugliness.

TONY. I know. There's this Complex at the back of us, it takes away all the light . . .

HEATHER. Exactly. Architecture.

She drinks.

(*Confidential.*) You see – personally – I don't believe that number of people died. In the gas chambers. I don't believe it's *humanly possible* for that number of people to die.

TONY. I don't believe it either. I never have.

HEATHER. It can't be.

,

Which isn't to trivialise. You see, Anthony, I think that if – like Lawrence – if you stare at ugly things for long enough, you get ugly yourself, inside. We need to show people the beautiful things. Those are the things we need to show to our children.

TONY. We need to wake up.

HEATHER. Wake up. That's beautiful. Yes.

,

Shall I tell you what I really like? I really like visiting stately homes. I've got a kind of season ticket and at the weekends I just take off. I just take off to a stately home . . .

TONY. Woburn Abbey . . .

HEATHER. The big ones naturally. But also when you apply you get a list of all the smaller ones nobody knows. So mostly it's those I visit. And that's the most beautiful thing. The most beautiful thing is to sit in one of those rooms and imagine it's mine. The plasterwork, the marble fireplaces, the gilding. Things that've lasted for hundreds of years. Mahogany floors. Do you think that's wrong?

TONY. No.

HEATHER. No it's not wrong. I know it's not wrong because I feel at home there, Anthony. What it is is a sense of confidence, of order. I can breathe. I say to myself: yes, this is me. You walk out in the gardens and what strikes you is the symmetry. Boxwood hedges. Pineapples made of stone. Round the walls there are fruit trees growing along wires. Figs. Morello cherries. Plums. In some of them they're recreating the past exactly. They're growing the same plants . . . the same species of plants. In the same places. As they were then. The same trees.

TONY. That's extraordinary.

HEATHER. So not just the house but the whole landscape is as it would've been. (*She drinks*.) I'm not making myself clear.

TONY. You are. Yes you are. Landscapes. That's exactly how it should be.

HEATHER. And it makes me think, it makes me think, Anthony, that if we could wear those clothes . . .

TONY. Uh-hu . . .

HEATHER. Or speak, speak as they did . . .

TONY. Like a person of that time . . . Speak poetry . . .

HEATHER. Because don't you ever get the feeling that the words we use . . .

TONY. We can't express ourselves . . .

HEATHER. . . . . that the words we use are just the shadow of a language that we've lost. And perhaps if we could speak that language . . .

TONY. I know . . .

HEATHER. Speak poetry . . . Or dance . . .

TONY. Yes . . .

HEATHER. They could all dance . . . (*She puts down her cup and offers her hand.*) Come on.

TONY. What?

HEATHER. We can dance.

TONY. Dance.

HEATHER. Yes. Come on.

TONY. You mean dance. You mean actually dance?

'

Now.

HEATHER. I mean actually dance. Yes.

TONY (*faint laugh*). I can't.

HEATHER. You can. (*She takes his hand.*) Of course you can. Why should we be limited by preconceived ideas about ourselves?

They begin to dance, without close physical contact, oddly graceful. HEATHER repeatedly hums a short slow phrase, and TONY joins in this ostinato. Time passes before HEATHER speaks.

In summer they have concerts. They play the music on the old instruments, the original instruments.

They continue to dance and hum.

Perhaps that's where we met.

'

TONY. Where?

HEATHER. In one of those houses, one of those rooms. In a previous life.

Both faint laugh. The dance continues until TONY breaks gently away.

TONY. I need a piss.

They both laugh. While TONY finds a dark corner, HEATHER, still humming the tune, leans against a wall.

HEATHER. Bonjour Mademoiselle. (*Faint laugh.*)

She continues to hum. TONY returns into the light. He drains the bottle into his mouth. Taking the bottle he goes to **HEATHER** *and presses himself against her.*

TONY. Let's do it.

HEATHER. What are you doing?

TONY. Come on. Let's do it.

HEATHER. What're you talking about?

It takes a moment for **HEATHER** *to realise that* **TONY** *is in earnest. But there is no question of an ambiguous response: she is utterly terrified.*

Get off me. What're you doing?

TONY. Shut up. Let's just do it.

HEATHER. Oh Jesus Christ.

TONY. Come on.

HEATHER. SOMEBODY HELP ME!

They struggle.

TONY. Come on. Ease up. Relax.

He pins her against the wall.

Come on. Pull this up. Help me. Pull it up. You're not helping me.

HEATHER. Oh Christ you're ripping . . . Help me he's insane.

TONY. You see the mistake I made last time . . . I frightened you by being weak. I'm sorry.

HEATHER. Just fuck off of me, fuck off . . .

TONY. I respected you as a *person* . . .

HEATHER. Help me . . .

TONY. What I failed to see last time was that – KEEP STILL – was that I needed to assert myself . . .

HEATHER. What d'you mean last time? What d'you mean?

TONY. But this time. Look. I'm in control. Ease up, Heather. Relax. Pull this up . . .

HEATHER. Please. It's a mistake . . .

TONY. I love you. I'm in control . . .

HEATHER. Look, you're confusing me with someone. We've never met . . .

TONY. No no no. You don't understand . . .

HEATHER. I do. I do understand, Anthony. Yes if we could just think about this, if we could just decide, just decide who it is –

TONY. KEEP STILL CAN'T YOU FUCK YOU!

He smashes the bottle against the wall. HEATHER *turns her head away in terror and closes her eyes, too afraid of the glass to fight. This sudden passivity confuses* TONY.

What's wrong? Your eyes are shut. What's wrong?

HEATHER. Just do it. Please, please don't hurt me. Just do it. Just do it and go away.

TONY. What d'you mean?

HEATHER *(eyes shut)*. I haven't seen you. I swear I can't describe you. Don't hurt me.

TONY. What d'you mean? We've been talking. We've been dancing. What d'you mean you can't describe me?

HEATHER *cannot speak.*

TONY. Open your eyes. OPEN YOUR EYES! *(He drops the piece of bottle and forces her eyes open.)* Look. It's me. Don't you remember me? This is me. Anthony. I want to marry you. We're going to have children.

HEATHER *spits in his face.*

TONY. You don't mean that. I'm sorry but you don't mean that. Yes yes yes last time we missed our chance, and perhaps you feel strongly, but now it's different: I'm in control.

HEATHER *slips away.*

Or we could have a meal.

'

We could have a meal. We could talk.

Blackout.

ACT TWO

1

A launderette. TONY *is folding shirts. Sitting apart from him is a black* MAN *wearing a shabby suit and tie, holding a briefcase. When this* MAN *begins to speak – quietly but insistently –* TONY *will ignore him for as long as possible. Firstly however there is silence as* TONY *folds.*

MAN. Wherever we look we see a world in decay.

It may be in the silence of the forests.

It may be moral decay. It may be in our inability to say what moral means.

Or it may be disease. A shadow falling on our most intimate moments.

Whenever we turn the soil to plant or build we uncover shallow graves. At every step we stumble over bones.

We look to culture to make sense of this, only to find that what we call culture consists of faint distress signals emanating from the wreck of our beliefs.

As we feel our way forwards, we find less and less to hold on to. We are blind men climbing sheer smooth rock in the dark.

We are astonished when we calculate the enormity of the universe. We discover that the world consists almost entirely of time and space. Why then do we seem to have so little of either?

At every step we stumble over bones. We are surely reaching the point where it will not be possible to go on, but we choose to ignore it.

The train.

The train streaks into a mountain tunnel from which it will never emerge. Briefly there are faces at the window. The children are waving. The adults in the buffet are dithering over a selection of fresh sandwiches. White or brown. With salad or without. They are experiencing the illusion of choice.

TONY *meets his glance. Silence.*

I'm sorry I'm embarrassing you.

TONY *faint laugh.*

MAN. Those are mostly extracts from chapter seven. The reflections on culture are from the appendix.

TONY. I see.

MAN. It's a theme I would've liked to develop, given the time.

TONY. Uh-hu.

'

MAN. You have a particular way of folding your shirts.

'

One can't help noticing.

TONY. I've always done it this way.

MAN. Do you travel much by train?

TONY. Bus. Mostly by bus.

MAN. You've possibly heard of me.

TONY. Uh-hu. I don't think so.

MAN. You've possible heard of me: Bott. Lawrence Bott.

He grasps TONY's *hand.*

TONY. No. (*Vague recollection.*) Well no actually it does seem familiar.

LAWRENCE. Some years ago I published a book. You might've heard of it.

TONY. Uh-hu.

LAWRENCE. *A World in Decay.* You've possibly heard of it.

TONY. Sorry.

LAWRENCE. Don't be.

,

No, don't be. I published *A World in Decay* at my own
expense and distributed it with a trolley to small
bookshops on a sale or return basis. Most of the copies
were in fact returned. No, don't be sorry.

TONY. No, I'm sorry.

LAWRENCE. Don't be.

,

Listen. I'd like to show you something.

He rummages in his briefcase as he speaks.

You see a crucial experience for me was my period at the
Adult Institute in Crossley Road. I was very moved by
what I saw there. I was moved and angered. Across the
corridor for example – in room D6 – there were grown
men and women struggling to read and write. I wanted
to weep for the opportunities that had been denied to
them. Their ambition, their ambition was often no more
than to recognise their own names.

He gives TONY *a card.*

And in my own classes – before their unfortunate closure
– I taught history three times a week, which was enough
to live on, in D17 – Lawrence Bott, you might've heard
of me – in those classes, whose closure is still subject to
appeal, in those classes, where I had expected from
adults at least a sense of the cumulative horror, I found
instead a calm acceptance of the past coupled with the
idea that it was a kind of never-ending classic serial, with
no expense spared on costume and the reconstruction of
period detail. There was no outrage. There was no
remorse. So what I did – and do you believe this is
wrong? – because how can it be wrong? – what I did was
I began to show them, methodically, whatever footage I
could find: of Dresden, of Hiroshima, of the crematoria
of Europe. I pointed out to them the terrible errors and
misunderstandings of History, which with hindsight are
so simply identified. I asked them to consider the

possibility – merely the possibility – that other choices might've been made. Better choices. But no: to them the past was like a film: frame followed frame: because it was inevitable, it justified itself. Justified. Now that made me really angry. I would say to them: are you seriously trying to tell me that these things were meant to be? That in other words they are part of a plan? Because if you are, if you are, don't you realise you're saying exactly the same as these fascists were, with their theories of biological superiority, of biological destiny. Are you seriously suggesting that these things were intended? That they serve a purpose? How can we accept that?

,

TONY. Look, it's very interesting, but really I just came in here to dry my shirts.

LAWRENCE. How can we accept that? Please don't trivialise.

TONY *contemplates the card.*

TONY. So what is this?

LAWRENCE. Yes yes yes. It may not be rational. But what has reason achieved? Reason has constructed the train. It has constructed the tunnel. What it has failed to provide is an exit.

TONY. Yes but what is this?

LAWRENCE. This is what I'm talking about.

TONY. Which is?

LAWRENCE. Not just History. But you as a person. The opportunities you've missed. The things you regret.

TONY. Which are?

LAWRENCE. Why should frame follow frame?

TONY. Which are?

LAWRENCE. You know what they are.

,

They're there in your eyes. From your earliest memory. You know what they are. Because what do we accumulate?

TONY (*increasingly absorbed in the card*). What is this exactly?

LAWRENCE. We accumulate wisdom only to find it's too late to apply it.

TONY. Bring this number . . .

LAWRENCE. Ring. It's a misprint. Please ring.

TONY. Uh-hu. A Marabout. What is that?

LAWRENCE. Mouhamed Lamine is a holy man and a personal friend.

TONY. Uh-hu.

'

Mouhamed Lamine.

LAWRENCE. He does not inhabit the world in a material sense.

TONY. Action at a distance . . .

LAWRENCE. Bending spoons.

TONY. Spoons.

LAWRENCE. That's just an example, a trivial example of what could be achieved.

'

Don't you see what I'm saying? If only we could go back.

Our language tells us that this is possible: what could've been, what might've been. These are the tenses of remorse and regret, but also the tenses of endless possibility.

If only we could go back.

Yes. Knowing what we do now.

Our language, if not our reason, tells us that this is possible.

'

(*Passionately.*) Look at us. We're not meant to be like this. We're human beings.

TONY. Speak for yourself.

LAWRENCE. We're human beings.

Silence.

TONY. Can I keep this?

LAWRENCE. The card is yours. I make no charge for the card.

TONY. Thankyou.

LAWRENCE. Thankyou for listening.

LAWRENCE *grasps* TONY's *hand between his, and holds onto it.*

Do you have twenty pence?

TONY. For the drier.

LAWRENCE. For me. For a human being. Do you have twenty pence?

TONY. But you –

LAWRENCE. I have nothing.

TONY. But you teach –

LAWRENCE. Teach? They won't even let me past reception. They're taking evidence. They're preparing reports.

TONY. No, that's terrible.

LAWRENCE. I'm in here to keep *warm*.

TONY (*reaches into pocket*). Twenty pence. No, that's really terrible. I'm sorry.

LAWRENCE. Don't be. Or whatever you can spare. Forty. Fifty. With fifty I can get chips. With a pound I could obtain a Special Brew, a Carlsberg Special Brew.

TONY. A pound.

LAWRENCE. Fifty pence. Whatever. Whatever you can spare. Thankyou.

TONY. It's nothing.

LAWRENCE. For another pound let me present you with a signed copy of my book.

LAWRENCE *gives a book to* TONY *who reads from the cover.*

TONY. A World in Decay. Thankyou.

LAWRENCE. It represents a considerable discount over the published price.

TONY *pays for the book, slips* LAMINE's *card inside, and pockets it.*

I realise this is embarrassing for you, but equally it is embarrassing for me. Please don't imagine I'm acting out of choice. When you have time, read it.

TONY. No. Thankyou. I will.

LAWRENCE. Bott. Lawrence Bott. You might've heard of me.

TONY. I have to go.

LAWRENCE. I'm in here to keep warm.

TONY. I'm sorry but I have to go now.

LAWRENCE. I accept that.

,

TONY. I have to take back these shirts and put them in a drawer.

LAWRENCE. Of course. I accept that.

,

Blackout.

2

The pub. NICK *plays the fruit-machine.* TONY *sits in the shadows staring at or through* KATE, *who is also lost in thought. Eventually he comes over to her, indifferent to the fact that she ignores him.*

TONY. No, I see what this must look like, but it isn't what you think. I mean I'm not making a play for you or anything. I'm aware that you have commitments and I respect that. If I'm drawn to you – and I am – it's because I'm drawn to you as a couple. You make a very attractive couple. (*As if she were about to speak.*) No, please, I think these things should be said.

,

I've always thought: I know her from somewhere, we've met. We've spoken before. But now I see that what it is is you're very like somebody. You've heard that before. Of course. But you genuinely are. You're genuinely like Franky where I work. Which is short for Frances. By which I don't mean to belittle you. Because of course you're unique. We're all of us unique. I'm just talking about a resemblance.

,

Perhaps I'm intruding – and if I am forgive me – but I've been doing a lot of thinking this evening. I've been sitting over there. You've probably noticed me. It's where I normally sit. I've been thinking about the past, and watching you both, and I find myself drawn.

,

I've been trying to think of my earliest memory. What's your earliest memory? I think mine is wearing red plastic sandals. It's summer and I'm wearing red plastic sandals. I'm looking at the sky and I notice that it's full of little bright specks, like sparks.

,

I asked my teacher: what are the little bright specks I can see? She told me: those are germs.

,

Do you think she really believed they were germs?

Faint smile from KATE, *who looks at him for the first time.*

And if not, what was she trying to do to me? I'd like to ask her that.

,

You see I've been watching you both. Not in that sense. No if I wanted to watch that – which I don't – I could go and pay for it. But I've been watching you both, and what I observe is that you don't talk to each other.

Which perhaps means that you don't need to – which is
all very well – it's all very well, but it makes me curious.
And stop me, please stop me if you feel I'm intruding
but it makes me curious as to what you really feel.

,

You don't talk. Now maybe that's love. I'd like to think
so. But maybe there's something else. Something that
eats away at you inside. That's all. I only ask because I'm
curious as to what you really feel. Perhaps it eats away at
you. And maybe if you talked . . .

,

Because you're welcome to come back. Both of you are
welcome to come back with me and talk. It's a small
place, but if you don't mind sitting on the bed . . .

NICK *has joined them.*

NICK. Excuse me.

TONY. This isn't what you think.

NICK. Excuse me.

,

TONY. No, I just want to talk. I'm not . . . listen, I'm not
suggesting anything.

NICK. You want to talk.

TONY. To both of you.

NICK. We're not interested.

TONY. This isn't what you think.

NICK. How d'you know what I think?

TONY. I mean if it was sexual . . .

NICK. How d'you know what I think?

TONY. I'm not saying I *know*.

NICK. Then what are you saying?

TONY. That's not what I'm saying.

,

NICK. Has he been saying anything to you?

KATE *shrugs*.

TONY. For example: perhaps you want children, but are unable to.

NICK. You're joking.

TONY. Maybe that's why you don't talk to each other . . .

NICK. Listen . . .

TONY. . . . ie there's a void . . .

NICK. Listen . . .

TONY. . . . or maybe you look at the world and say: what right do we have? I can understand that.

NICK. Crap.

TONY. Because we're blind. We're climbing rocks in the dark.

NICK. Crap.

TONY. I respect that. Alright. I respect that.

NICK. There's nothing wrong with the *world*.

TONY. OK.

,

OK. I respect that. It's debatable. But if that's so – maybe it's so – but let me ask you a question.

NICK. You want to ask me a question.

TONY. Yes. What is there that you regret?

NICK. What?

TONY. What do you regret?

,

NICK. Nothing.

TONY. What d'you mean nothing?

NICK. I mean nothing.

KATE *and* NICK *exchange a faint laugh.*

TONY. No, listen: I'm talking about the things you've done in your life.

NICK. Right. So what's wrong with your life?

TONY. No, I'm not asking you . . .

NICK. I know that.

TONY. . . . to tell me, to tell me what's wrong with my life.

NICK. I know that.

,

So let's leave it.

TONY. What I'm asking you is if you've ever regretted anything. Yourself as a person.

NICK. As a person.

TONY. Because I'm not asking you to tell me what's wrong with my life. Because alright I know what's wrong with it. I have insight into that.

NICK. Uh-hu.

,

You're taking it too seriously.

TONY. What?

NICK. You're taking it –

TONY. My life. I'm taking it too seriously.

NICK. You've put your finger on it.

TONY. Well thankyou very much.

,

NICK. There you are.

TONY. Thankyou very much.

NICK. There you are. Look at yourself. You're taking it too seriously.

TONY. Well thankyou. Fuck you as a matter of fact.

NICK. That's fine.

TONY. Fuck you.

,

NICK. My pleasure.

TONY. Because whoever you are . . .

KATE. All the world's a stage.

TONY. . . . you're not in a position to pass judgement.

NICK. Really.

KATE. We're actors. The world's a stage.

TONY. I'm sorry, but that's a meaningless remark.

NICK. She's right.

KATE. We strut. We fret.

NICK. She's right.

TONY. No, I'm sorry but she isn't right. How can that be right? I mean this isn't an act. This is me. I'm here. I'm making decisions. I could've stayed over there where I normally sit but no I've come over here of my own free will to speak to you both because I have something to say. An actor is repeating a part, but this is different, this is entirely different.

'

This is significant. This is me.

KATE. It's a tale told by an idiot.

TONY. Is that supposed to be a comment?

KATE. Signifying nothing.

TONY. Is that supposed to be some kind of a comment?

'

Well is it?

NICK. Leave it.

KATE. It's actually poetry.

NICK. Let's leave it.

TONY. Poetry.

NICK. This is an actress. You're talking to an actress.

'

TONY. What's that – a professional actress?

KATE. I'm Kate. Yes.

TONY. I'm sorry. Hello Kate.

KATE. Hello.

TONY. Anthony. And I apologise. Because I respect your profession.

KATE. Thankyou.

TONY. But as an actress – whatever kind of actress you are – I know that you'll have insight into human nature.

NICK. I'll tell you what I do regret.

'

TONY. Because that's your job.

NICK. I'll tell you what I do regret.

TONY. I'd like you to.

NICK. What I regret, my friend, is the fact that you exist.

KATE *laughs and puts her arm around* NICK.

KATE. He doesn't mean that.

TONY. No that's absolutely fine by me. Because I take that –

NICK. Don't I?

TONY. I take that in the spirit in which it was intended.

NICK. No offence.

TONY. That is to say ie as an example. A trivial example. Absolutely. None taken.

NICK *and* KATE *kiss.* TONY *continues as if he had their attention.*

Because no one's denying, Kate, that we learn from our mistakes. And I accept your point that a poet can turn that into poetry. That's fine. But for the rest of us who are not poets which is the vast majority, by the time we've learned from our mistakes it's already too late. Those opportunities will never return. And even if you study life, even if you write books about it, you can still find yourself in the launderette, not to do your washing, I mean just to keep *warm.*

KATE *slips away.*

Where's she going?

NICK. What d'you mean?

TONY. Katy. Where's Katy going?

NICK. She's going to the toilet.

TONY. OK. Fine.

NICK. She's just going to the toilet.

TONY. No, that's fine.

,

Listen –

NICK. You have something against that?

TONY. No. Listen. How old am I?

NICK (*shrugs*). Forty?

TONY. How did you know that?

,

That's exactly right. I'm thirty-nine, and tomorrow I'll be forty.

NICK. Crisis in other words.

TONY. No, are you psychic?

NICK. Congratulations.

TONY. What? No. Not congratulations.

NICK. OK.

TONY. Not congratulations, because . . .

,

Because. Alright?

NICK. Because.

TONY. Because I will be forty years old tomorrow, and over those forty years, what have I accumulated?

NICK (*shrugs*). Money?

TONY. Money, no.

,

No I'm not speaking in a material sense.

NICK. Give up.

TONY. Wisdom.

NICK. Wisdom.

TONY. Yes, we accumulate wisdom, but what use is it to us? Because the events when the wisdom would've been useful, they're over and gone.

NICK. Well then that's how it is.

TONY. No that's *not* how it is.

NICK. Well then I'm sorry, I don't understand what you're saying.

TONY. That's alright.

,

No that's alright. I accept that because what I'm trying to say is not rational.

NICK. It's not rational.

TONY. No.

,

NICK. Fine.

TONY. I mean how old are you?

,

NICK. Why? Twenty-eight.

TONY. And what's your profession?

NICK. My profession?

TONY. Yes, what do you do?

NICK. Do I have a job?

TONY. Yes.

NICK (*faint laugh*). No.

TONY. In other words you missed the opportunity. The opportunity was there, but at the crucial moment you said to yourself: this isn't me.

NICK. What opportunity?

TONY. To work. To get a job. Because if that opportunity presented itself again – and what I'm suggesting to you is that that could be possible – you wouldn't say: this isn't me. You'd seize it. You wouldn't be coming here . . .

NICK. I happen to like coming here . . .

TONY. Night after night.

NICK. I like coming here.

TONY. You like coming here.

'

Don't deceive yourself.

KATE *returns.*

Don't deceive yourself. You and Katy here make an attractive couple, as I was saying. But why does an attractive couple come in here night after night to drink this stuff and sit in basically silence?

'

NICK. It's Anthony's birthday.

KATE. Congratulations Anthony.

TONY. Tomorrow. Thankyou.

KATE. Are you doing anything?

TONY. Tomorrow? Not doing as such. No.

As TONY *drains his glass,* KATE *whispers to* NICK.

NICK (*prompted by* KATE). Look, d'you want another drink, Tone?

TONY. Sorry?

NICK. Your birthday. You want a – ?

KATE. Well of course he does.

TONY. A drink? Well yes, if you're . . .

NICK. Pils?

TONY. Holsten Pils. Thankyou very much.

NICK. This dead?

TONY. Thanks. Thanks a lot.

> NICK *goes with the empties. Silence punctuated by faint fruit-machine.*

> Fantastic. You look fantastic.

> KATE *faint laugh.*

TONY. You have a lovely face.

KATE. Thankyou.

TONY. Have I said that before?

KATE. No.

TONY. Because I know I have a habit, I know I've a habit of repeating myself.

KATE. You didn't say that before.

TONY. Good, that's good. You have a lovely face.

KATE. Thankyou.

TONY. You have a lovely face, but you've still failed. Why is that?

KATE (*faint laugh*). I haven't failed.

TONY. Of course you've failed. Look.

KATE. What?

TONY. It's there in your eyes.

KATE. Listen, I –

TONY. I didn't want to say that but it's there in your eyes, Kate. What does an actress do in the evenings? An actress works. She's known. I mean Kate what? Kate who? If you weren't here what difference would it make to anything? And naturally you persuade yourself that there is an intention, that it's meant to be like this, it's meant to be. But what does meant to be mean? Meant to be doing the same thing for eighteen years? Meant to be keeping warm next to a clothes-drier while someone writes reports? No way.

No way, Kate. Meant to be means nothing.

KATE. What reports?

TONY. Because listen, what are we, you and I?

KATE. Wait a minute, wait a minute. Don't include me in this.

TONY. We're human beings.

KATE. Don't include me.

TONY. We're human beings. And perhaps I'm repeating myself, but for human beings everything should be possible. The language we speak tells us that. It tells us that the potential – by which I mean not only what we could be, but what we might've been – the potential is infinite. And so what's *meant* to happen – which is surely the realisation of that potential – are you with me? – what's meant to happen, hasn't happened. And what *has* happened – what's happened to *us* – was not meant to happen. No.

,

How can we believe that about ourselves? Because listen –

KATE. I'm listening.

TONY. OK.

,

Yes?

KATE. I'm listening to you.

TONY. Good.

KATE. No, I'm interested.

TONY. Well you should be.

KATE. I am. What are you suggesting?

TONY. That's good. Because listen, I normally sit over there and every night I see you, the two of you, over here, and don't you understand my heart bleeds.

KATE. And if I happen to like it here?

TONY. It bleeds for you. What d'you mean: like it here? That's exactly what *he* said. (*Picks up a bottle.*) Don't you know what this stuff is doing to your body? If you got pregnant? What sort of baby you might have?

KATE (*betraying sadness*). That's unlikely.

TONY. Exactly.

,

Yes, exactly.

KATE. So what are you suggesting?

TONY (*intensely*). What I'm suggesting, Kate, is that there is a train. It's going into the tunnel. The children are waving.

,

I'm suggesting that if we could only go *back*.

,

KATE *faint laugh.*

TONY. Yes.

KATE. You can't go back.

TONY. Yes, but if only we could. Live our lives again. Knowing what we do now. Knowing that. Don't you see?

As NICK *approaches with new bottles,* TONY *takes a piece of paper from his pocket and passes it to* KATE.

KATE. What's this?

TONY. No, look at it.

While NICK *gives* TONY *a bottle,* KATE *unfolds the paper.*

Cheers.
That's right. Look at it.

NICK. What is it?

KATE (*reads*). 'Custom Coils Farringdon Road. Friendly family firm requires . . .'

TONY. No no no . . .

KATE. '. . . requires supervisor for specialist workshop.' So?

TONY. Not that. I don't mean that.

TONY *feels in his pockets. He gets out the book.*

KATE (*to* NICK). Have you seen the date on this? Look: it's falling apart.

TONY. I don't mean that. I had a card. He gave me a card.

KATE. 'Telephone Frances Wood.'

NICK *has hold of the book.*

TONY. Mouhamed Lamine. It was in there.

NICK (*reads*). 'Wherever we look we see a world in decay.'

KATE (*laughs*). What?

NICK. 'It may be in the silence of the forests. It may be moral decay.'

TONY. It was in there.

NICK. 'It may be in our inability to say what moral means.'

NICK *laughs and tosses down the book.*

TONY. No. Lamine. Mouhamed Lamine.

KATE. Gave you the book?

TONY. No. A card. He gave me a card. Lawrence gave me a card. It was in there.

NICK. How can you read that stuff?

TONY. It was in there.

NICK. Well don't look at me.

Don't look at me.

TONY. Will you please return it.

NICK. What?

TONY. Yes. I'm asking you to return my card.

NICK (*walking away*). What card? I'm sorry but I don't believe this. This is not in fact happening.

TONY. You're not walking away. You're not walking away with something that is mine by rights.

NICK. Will someone please tell this person –

TONY. DON'T WALK AWAY FROM ME!

TONY seizes NICK. A brief but very violent struggle. NICK produces a knife and stabs TONY dead. After a short silence KATE realises that the knife has fallen.

KATE (*softly*). Pick it up.

NICK (*faint laugh of disbelief*). Something so trivial . . .

KATE. Pick it up.

'

NICK (*with difficulty*). I don't regret this.
    Why do people have to talk?

With great reluctance, KATE recovers the knife.

What makes them start conversations? What do they
expect to achieve?
What's wrong?

KATE. Just take it. (*She gives him the knife.*)

NICK. I like coming here. I like *being* here.

'

I don't regret this. There's nothing wrong with the *world*.
The man is dreaming.

KATE tries to move NICK away.

KATE. Come on.

NICK. Don't patronise me. Don't patronise me. I'm in
control.

KATE. Yes yes yes. Alright. Come on.

NICK. I am. I'm in control. (*Faint laugh.*)

KATE. I know. Come on. Move.

'

Move now.

Neither moves.

Blackout.

3

Lights come up bright at Custom Coils. Supervisor **MARC** *is
inspecting stock, making notes on a clipboard, taking his time. His
back is turned to* **BARBARA** *who stacks boxes of components. Both
wear surgical hats. The phone is ringing. For a while no one speaks.*

BARBARA. Marc.

Marc, it's the phone.

Phone continues to ring.

MARC. Will you answer the phone.

BARBARA (*quietly rising hysteria*). Marc. I'm busy. I'm
trying to do this.

I can't be in two places at once, Marc. The phone isn't
my responsibility. I'm trying to do this. I haven't slept all
night. I'm upset. I've had nightmares. I called the doctor
but it was just a recorded message. Then you ask me to
answer the phone. I mean are you trying to make me
overdose again, Marc? Is that what you're trying to do?

Phone continues to ring. MARC's *back remains turned.*

Do you want to have that on your conscience? Because I
feel very close to it this morning. I feel very close to it,
Marc. And all it needs is for people to start making
demands –

BARBARA *drops a box. She exclaims and immediately begins to
cry. The components scatter.* MARC *takes no obvious notice of
this. After a moment he goes and answers the phone.*

MARC. Custom Coils . . .

But the caller has hung up. MARC *replaces the receiver. He
contemplates* BARBARA, *then goes up to her.*

(*Gently.*) Barbara . . . Barbara . . .

He takes out a handkerchief. BARBARA *takes it and wipes her
eyes. She looks up. They both smile. She clutches his arm. They
separate and return to their tasks,* BARBARA *putting the
components back in the box.*

TERRY *enters, in surgical hat.*

TERRY. Morning.

No reaction from MARC *or* BARBARA. TERRY *takes a piece of paper out of his pocket.*

(Tentatively.) Marc . . . when you have time, mate . . . perhaps we could . . . go over this together. OK?

,

So what is this then? A minute's silence or what?

FRANKY *enters. She lights a cigarette.* TERRY *helps* BARBARA *clear up. This proceeds in silence.* FRANKY *makes one or two aimless moves: there's no reason for her to be in the room. After a while she takes a magazine from under a pair of ear-cans.*

FRANKY. Country Life? *(Faint laugh.)* Whose is this?

BARBARA. It's Tony's.

,

FRANKY. Tony's. Uh-hu. Right.

,

TERRY. Yes he was cutting out pictures, wasn't he.

FRANKY. Was he.

BARBARA. He was cutting out pictures of houses. Stately homes.

BARBARA, TERRY *and* MARC *all exchange a glance at this. A faint laugh ripples round.*

FRANKY. No music.

,

TERRY. So what, you going to . . . you going to advertise?

BARBARA. For godsake Terry . . .

,

FRANKY. Advertise, no, I think we're managing. That's right, isn't it Marc: we're managing?

MARC. That's right. We're managing.

FRANKY. Good.

Managing, no, that's very good. Let's have some music, Terry.

TERRY *moves to the radio.*

BARBARA. I've just been telling Marc, Miss Wood, I still can't sleep. I have nightmares, recurring nightmares, and when you ring the doctor all you get is an answering machine. I'm wondering how long I can go on, how long I can –

The radio cuts her off: a loud driving rhythm that prevents conversation. FRANKY smokes, remains in the room. The others resume their tasks. They surrender to the relentless optimism of the music.